Military DOGS

by Frances E. Ruffin

**Consultant: Wilma Melville, Founder
National Disaster Search Dog Foundation**

BEARPORT
PUBLISHING

New York, New York

Special thanks to Wilma Melville who founded the:
National Disaster Search Dog Foundation
206 N. Signal Street, Suite R
Ojai, CA 93023
(888) 4K9-HERO
www.SearchDogFoundation.org

The Search Dog Foundation is a not-for-profit organization that rescues dogs, gives them professional training, and partners them with firefighters to find people buried alive in disasters. They produce the most highly trained search dogs in the nation.

To Col. Melvin S. Smith,
United States Army, Ret.

Credits

Cover and Title Page, © Christopher Walkenhorst, United States Air Force; Cover (RT), © United States Coast Guard photo by PA3 Constantina Mourtos; Cover (RM), © Bettmann/CORBIS; Cover (RB), © United States Air Force photo by Airman 1st Class Bradley A. Lail; Table of Contents, © Mario Tama/Getty Images; Page 4, © United States Air Force; 6, © Vietnam Security Police Association, Inc., courtesy of Bill Cummings; 7, © courtesy, Lt. Colonel Robert M. Sullivan; 8, © Pierre Colombel/CORBIS; 9, © Mary Evans Picture Library; 10, © History of Technology Division, National Museum of American History, Smithsonian Institution; 11, © Bettmann/CORBIS; 12, © United States Coast Guard Historian's Office Photo Collection; 13, © Bettmann/CORBIS; 14, © Courtesy of The Library of Virginia; 15, © The National Archives; 16, © The Art Archive / Culver Pictures; 17, © The Art Archive / Culver Pictures; 18, © Spc. Katherine M. Roth, U.S. Army / Department of Defense; 19, © United States Air Force photo by Airman 1st Class Bradley A. Lail; 20, © Master Sgt. Scott Wagers, United States Air Force; 22, © Master Sgt. Scott Wagers, United States Air Force; 23, © Luis Santana; 24, © Cpl. Sarah A. Beavers, United States Marine Corps; 25, © Mario Tama/Getty Images; 26, © United States Air Force photo by Dennis Plummer; 27, © United States Coast Guard photo by PA3 Constantina Mourtos; 29T, © Photodisc / Fotosearch.com; 29M, © Arco Images / Alamy; 29B, © Yann Arthus-Bertrand/CORBIS.

Publisher: Kenn Goin
Project Editor: Lisa Wiseman
Creative Director: Spencer Brinker
Original Design: Dawn Beard Creative

Library of Congress Cataloging-in-Publication Data

Ruffin, Frances E.
  Military dogs / by Frances E. Ruffin.
    p. cm. — (Dog heroes)
  Includes bibliographical references and index.
  ISBN-13: 978-1-59716-273-9 (library binding)
  ISBN-10: 1-59716-273-6 (library binding)
  ISBN-13: 978-1-59716-301-9 (pbk.)
  ISBN-10: 1-59716-301-5 (pbk.)
  1. Dogs—War use—Juvenile literature. I. Title. II. Series.

UH100.R84 2007
355.4'24—dc22

2006004372

For more information, write to Bearport Publishing Company, Inc., 101 Fifth Avenue, Suite 6R, New York, New York 10003. Printed in the United States of America in North Mankato, Minnestoa.

062010
052810-Dog Heroes

10 9 8 7 6 5

Table of Contents

A Hidden Enemy

Just after midnight, more than 60 enemy soldiers secretly surrounded a U.S. air base in Vietnam. They waited for the right moment to attack.

U.S. soldiers couldn't see or hear the enemy. A **sentry** dog named Rebel, however, knew something was wrong. He began barking and pulling on his leash. When his **handler** let him go, the dog ran into the darkness. His handler called for help, but it was too late. A rain of bullets killed Rebel.

A few hours later, another sentry dog named Toby picked up the enemies' **scent**. He **alerted** his handler, who then warned other U.S. soldiers. Though Toby was killed, several enemy soldiers were caught. The danger seemed to be over.

41051

The attack on the Tan Son Nhut Air Base took place in 1966 during the war with Vietnam, a country in Asia.

Tan Son Nhut Air Base

A Hero Named Nemo

The next night, a large German shepherd named Nemo and his handler, Bob, stood watch at the base. Like the other U.S. soldiers, Bob thought the enemy had been caught the night before.

Nemo

Then Nemo suddenly sensed danger. Seconds later, an enemy soldier opened fire. Nemo charged toward the blast and was shot under the eye. As Bob tried to fight the other soldiers, he was shot, too. Bleeding, Nemo crawled over to Bob and covered the soldier's body with his own. By protecting him until help arrived, Nemo saved Bob's life.

Sentry Dog "NEMO" A534

On 4 December 1966, Sentry Dog, NEMO, engaged the enemy during an attack on Tan Son Nhut Air Base, Republic of Viet Nam. Though severely wounded he saved the life of his wounded handler, and helped to prevent a successful attack of that installation.

Dogs and their handlers may have saved the lives of more than 10,000 soldiers during the Vietnam War.

Captain Robert Sullivan holds one of Nemo's many awards.

In Peace and in War

Dogs and humans have lived together for thousands of years. Cave people often hunted with their dogs. At night, the dogs protected them by barking to scare off wild animals. The Greeks and the Romans were probably the first to use dogs in battle. Their animals even wore armor.

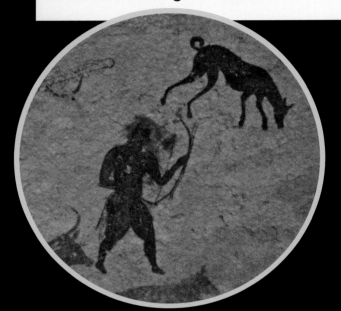

This painting shows a warrior hunting with his dog.

At one time, the British Army trained dogs to jump out of planes and land by parachute. These dogs were called "Parapups."

For the most part, however, people kept dogs as pets. Then in 1884, Germany started a school that trained dogs for its army. Later, in World War I (1914–1918), several countries in Europe began to use dogs for police as well as **military** work.

German dog handlers get their orders in 1898.

More Than a Mascot

During World War I, the United States didn't allow dogs in the military. However, that didn't stop soldiers from bringing their pets when they were shipped **overseas**.

In 1918, U.S. soldier Robert Conroy **smuggled** his pit bull, Stubby, aboard his **troop** ship. The ship was headed for France. First, Stubby became the troop's **mascot**. Then he became one of its heroes.

For his heroics, Stubby was awarded a gold medal by General John J. Pershing in 1921.

Late one night, the enemy attacked the troops with poison gas. Stubby barked loudly to wake the men. This warning gave them enough time to put on their gas masks. Another time, Stubby caught an enemy soldier by holding on to the man's pants with his teeth.

Stubby was in 17 battles. He was hurt several times. However, he always recovered and bravely returned to duty.

Stubby, wearing all of his medals, during a visit to the White House in 1924

Defense Dogs

Dogs were officially allowed in the U.S. military during World War II (1939–1945). In the beginning, the animals only patrolled the coastlines.

The Army, however, believed that dogs could also help defend the country during battle. The military started a program called Dogs for Defense.

U.S. Coast Guardsmen and their military dogs patrol the shores.

Americans were asked to **donate** their pets. More than 19,000 dogs were given to the military. The dogs had to be healthy. They had to pass tests to see if they were well behaved. They could not be frightened by the sound of guns or thunderstorms. In the end, about 10,000 animals were trained to become war dogs.

Even President Franklin Delano Roosevelt's dog, Fala, helped out during the war. He enlisted in the Army as a private.

The Dogs for Defense program first accepted more than 30 **breeds** of dogs. Today mostly German shepherds, Dutch shepherds, and Belgian Malinois are used in the military.

Guarding and Scouting

The military dogs of World War II had very important jobs. Sentry dogs guarded soldiers, vehicles, weapons, and important buildings. They were trained to attack. They were often ordered to rush into buildings and grab an enemy. At times, they were even commanded to kill. Such powerful animals could be difficult to handle. Sometimes they attacked harmless people.

World War II military officers training Buster, a sentry dog

Another job the dogs had was to locate enemy soldiers. These scout dogs traveled with their handlers ahead of the troops. When the animals spotted the enemy, they would quietly stand still, prick up their ears, and hold their tails stiff. Scout dogs were trained to tell the difference between friends and enemies.

Scout dogs during World War II

Andy was a sentry dog who could also scout. He not only guarded the base, but he went out with his **company** of marines. He became a World War II hero.

Other Jobs for War Dogs

Not all military dogs were used in battle. In World War I and World War II, some dogs carried messages between troops. Notes were put into little cans. The cans were then attached to the dogs' collars. Messenger dogs could sneak past the enemy and not get caught.

A soldier takes a note from a messenger dog's collar.

In addition to messages, some dogs also carried pigeons in small pouches on their backs. After the dog delivered the message, the soldier would write a reply. The reply was attached to the pigeon that then flew back to home base.

Soldiers training dogs to deliver messages

The U.S. Army also created war dog platoons in World War II. These groups usually had about 27 scout dogs, 6 messenger dogs, and 20 handlers and soldiers.

The Best War Dogs

Dogs make wonderful soldiers. They can find enemies using their great sense of smell. They can also hear sounds too high for human ears. For example, dogs can hear bombs before they explode. This ability allows them to warn soldiers to take cover before it's too late.

A German shepherd checks a car for bombs in Baghdad, Iraq.

Which breed makes the best dog soldier? Many military groups around the world prefer German shepherds. Their strength and large size make them great guard dogs. They're smart and can learn new skills easily, too. The military also likes these dogs because they can withstand very hot and cold temperatures. An undercoat of fur helps keep them warm in icy conditions. They shed the undercoat when the weather is hot.

Military dogs are tattooed with an identification number inside one of their ears. This number helps the military keep track of them.

Manzo, a German shepherd military dog

Military Dog School

Some people breed dogs for the military. The government pays about $4,000 for each dog. Before the dogs are purchased, they are carefully tested. They must be fit, have no health problems, and be well behaved. They also have to weigh at least 55 pounds (25 kg).

Only five weeks old, Lance, Lindy, and Leo are candidates for military dog training.

The dogs who pass the tests are sent to school. They learn all they need to know at the Military Working Dog Center at Lackland Air Force Base in San Antonio, Texas.

In 1998, Lackland started a puppy program where they breed their own dogs for their training school. Currently, the program has produced several litters of Belgian Malinois puppies.

Before dogs from the puppy program start training at Lackland, they live with a family for a few months. This helps them get used to being around people.

Training

Dogs are in military school for about 100 days. They are trained to stay calm in crowds and to let people come near them. They learn to spot the enemy and to attack on command. The dogs are also taught other skills, such as how to sniff for bombs.

Lacy Smith, who runs the puppy program at Lackland, works with four-month-old India.

While in training, the animals learn to work as a team with their handlers. When a dog performs well, he or she is rewarded with a toy and some playtime.

After training, the dogs are sent to the Air Force, Army, Navy, or Marine Corps. Some military dogs also work for the Secret Service. This group helps guard the president of the United States and his family.

Today, more than 2,300 military dogs work for the **Department of Defense.**

A Secret Service agent and her military dog patrol the White House.

Fighting Terrorism

Today's military dogs are helping to fight the war on **terrorism**. Some of them are even serving in the **Middle East**. There, they guard troops, search buildings for hidden enemies, and sniff for bombs.

Dogs serving in Iraq are given goggles to protect their eyes during sandstorms. They also wear special boots to keep their paws from being burned on the hot desert sand.

Military dogs also protect people and buildings in large cities around the United States. In fact, it's common to see soldiers and their dogs in airports and train stations. They may be searching for bombs or drugs.

A Metropolitan Transit policeman and his dog stand guard inside Penn Station in New York City. They are on the lookout for bombs.

Brave Soldiers

Most military dogs work for about ten years. Until recently, they were put to sleep when their active duty ended. People believed that the dogs were too **aggressive** and hard to handle to become pets. In 2000, however, President Bill Clinton signed a law that allows the handlers of these brave dogs to adopt them when they retire.

U.S. Air Force Technical Sergeant Jamie Dana and her bomb-sniffing dog, Rex, were in Iraq when they were injured. In 2006, President George W. Bush signed a bill that let Jamie adopt Rex even though he was still on active duty.

Military dogs are true heroes. They have been shot at by enemy fire and poisoned by gas. Thousands have died in the line of duty. Over and over again, these brave dogs have shown that they are true friends to the soldiers they serve and protect.

Petty Officer Chad Olson pets his military partner, Cisco.

Once military dogs retire, they are given special training before they are adopted. They need to learn how to live off the battlefield.

Just the Facts

- In World War I, dogs were taught to carry back the hats of injured soldiers to let others know that the men were badly hurt.

- Police dogs have only one handler during their working career. Military dogs may have several. When dog handlers leave the service or are killed, war dogs have to get used to new handlers.

- At one time, small dogs served as mascots on submarines. They were called "sea dogs."

- Scout dogs can smell an enemy soldier from 1,000 yards (914 m) away. They can even smell the breath of a spy who is underwater and breathing through a reed.

- U.S. Air Force Technical Sergeant Jamie Dana and her dog, Rex, were guests of First Lady Laura Bush at the State of the Union Speech in January 2006.

Common Breeds: MILITARY DOGS

German shepherd

Dutch shepherd

Belgian Malinois

aggressive (uh-GRESS-iv) forceful or angry

alerted (uh-LURT-id) warned someone of danger

breeds (BREEDZ) types of animals

company (KUHM-puh-nee) a group of soldiers serving under the same captain

Department of Defense (di-PART-muhnt UHV di-FENSS) part of the U.S. government that controls the Army, Navy, Air Force, and Marines

donate (DOH-nate) to give something away

handler (HAND-lur) someone who trains and works with animals

mascot (MASS-kot) an animal, person, or object that is supposed to bring good luck to a group of people.

Middle East (MID-uhl EEST) an area made up of several countries, including Iraq and Saudi Arabia, that covers parts of Asia and Africa

military (MIL-uh-*ter*-ee) having to do with the armed forces

overseas (*oh*-vur-SEEZ) traveling across the ocean to other countries

scent (SENT) the smell of a person or animal

sentry (SEN-tree) a person or animal who stands guard to warn others of danger

smuggled (SMUHG-uhld) secretly brought something

terrorism (TER-ur-iz-uhm) the use of threats or violence to scare and control other people

troop (TROOP) a group of soldiers

Bibliography

Bidner, Jen. *Dog Heroes: Saving Lives and Protecting America.* Guilford, CT: Lyons Press (2002).

Cooper, Jilly. *Animals in War: Valiant Horses, Courageous Dogs and Other Unsung Animal Heroes.* Guilford, CT: Lyons Press (2002).

Hamer, Blythe. *Dogs at War.* London: Carlton Books (2001).

Lemish, Michael G. *War Dogs: A History of Loyalty and Heroism.* Dulles, VA: Brassey's (1996).

Putney, Capt. William W. *Always Faithful: A Memoir of the Marine Dogs of World War II.* New York: The Free Press (2001).

Siegel, Mary-Ellen, and Hermine M. Koplin. *More Than a Friend: Dogs With a Purpose.* New York: Walker and Company (1984).

Read More

The American Kennel Club. *The Complete Dog Book for Kids.* New York: John Wiley (1996).

Clutton-Brock, Juliet. *Dog.* New York: DK Publishing (2000).

George, Jean Craighead. *How to Talk to Your Dog.* New York: Harper Collins (2000).

Lauber, Patricia. *The True-or-False Book of Dogs.* New York: Harper Collins (2003).

Learn More Online

Visit these Web sites to learn more about military dogs:

community-2.webtv.net/Hahn-50thAP-K9/K9History20/

library.thinkquest.org/CR0210580/bombsniffingbara.htm

usmilitary.about.com/od/jointservices/a/militarydogs.htm

www.militaryworkingdog.com/history

Index

About the Author

Frances E. Ruffin has written many nonfiction books for children.
She lives and writes in New York City.